A Word About

Pride

A Puritan Classic

By Richard Baxter

Richard Baxter

Originally entitled *A Word about Pride to All but Especially to Ministers of the Gospel*

Excerpted from the book "The Reformed Pastor"

A Word About Pride

One of our most heinous and palpable sins is PRIDE. This is a sin that hath too much interest in the best of us, but which is more hateful and inexcusable in us than in other men. Yet is it so prevalent in some of us, that it indicteth our discourses, it chooseth our company, it formeth our countenances, it putteth the accent and emphasis upon our words. It fills some men's minds with aspiring desires, and designs. It possesseth them with envious and bitter thoughts against those who stand in their light, or who by any means eclipse their glory, or hinder the progress of their reputation. Oh what a constant companion! what a tyrannical commander, what a sly and subtle insinuating enemy, is this sin of pride! It goes with men to the draper, the mercer, the tailor: it chooseth them their cloth, their trimming and their fashion. Fewer ministers would ruffle it out in the fashion in hair and habit, if it were not for the command of this tyrannous vice. And I would that this were all, or the worst. But, alas, how frequently doth PRIDE go with us to our study, and there sit with us and do our work! How oft doth it choose our subject, and, more frequently still, our words and ornaments!

God commandeth us to be as plain as we can, that we may inform the ignorant; and as convincing and serious as we are able, that we may melt and change their hardened hearts. But pride stands by and contradicteth all, and produceth its toys and trifles. It polluteth rather than polisheth. And, under presence of laudable ornaments, dishonoreth our sermons with childish things, as if a prince were to be decked in the habit of a stage-player, or a painted fool. Pride persuadeth us to paint the window, that it may dim the light, and to speak to our people that which they cannot understand, to let them know that we are able to speak unprofitably. If we have a plain and cutting passage, it taketh off the edge, and dulls the life of our preaching, under presence of filing off the roughness, unevenness, and superfluity.

When God chargeth us to deal with men as for their lives, and to beseech them with all the earnestness that we are able; this cursed sin controlleth all, and condemneth the most holy commands of God, and saith to us, 'What! Will you make people think you are mad? Will you make them say you rage or rave? Cannot you speak soberly and moderately?' And thus doth pride make many a man's sermons; and what pride makes the devil makes, and what sermons the devil will make and to what end, we may easily conjecture. Though the matter be of God, yet if the dress, and manner, and end be from Satan, we have no great reason to expect success.

And when pride hath made the sermon, it goes with us into the pulpit, formeth our tone, animateth us in the delivery, takes us off from that which may be displeasing, how necessary soever, and setteth us in pursuit of vain applause. In short, the sum of all is this; it maketh men, both in studying and preaching, to seek themselves, and deny God, when they should seek God's glory, and deny themselves.

When they should inquire, What shall I say, and how shall I say it, to please God best, and do most good? it makes them ask, What shall I say, and how shall I deliver it, to be thought a learned able preacher, and to be applauded by all that hear me? When the sermon is done, pride goeth home with them, and maketh them more eager to know whether they were applauded, than whether they did prevail for the saving of souls. Were it not for shame, they could find in their hearts to ask people how they liked them and to draw out their commendations. If they perceive that they are highly thought of, they rejoice, as having attained their end; but if they see that they are considered but weak or common men, they are displeased, as having missed the prize they had in view.

But even this is not all, nor the worst, if worse may be. Oh, that ever it should be said of godly ministers, that they are so set upon popular air, and on sitting highest in men's estimation; that they envy the talents and names of their brethren who are preferred before them. As if all were taken from their praise that is given to another; and as if God had given them his gifts to be the mere ornaments and trappings of their persons, that they may walk as men of reputation in the world, and as if all his gifts to others were to be trodden down and vilified, if they seem to stand in the way of their honor, What? A saint, a preacher of Christ, and yet envy that which hath the image of Christ, and malign his gifts for which he should have the glory, and all because they seem to hinder our glory?

Is not every true Christian a member of the body of Christ, and, therefore, partaketh of the blessings of the whole, and of each particular member thereof? And doth not every man owe thanks to God for his brethren's gifts, not only as having himself a part in them, as the foot hath the benefit of the guidance of the eye, but also because his own ends may be attained by his brethren's gifts, as well as by his own? For if the glory of God, and the Church's felicity, be not his end, he is not a Christian. Will any workman malign another, because he helpeth him to do his master's work? Yet, alas, how common is this heinous crime among the ministers of Christ!

They can secretly blot the reputation of those that stand in the way of their own; and what they cannot for shame do in plain and open terms, lest they be proved liars and slanderers, they will do in generals, and by malicious intimations, raising suspicions where they cannot fasten accusations. And some go so far, that they are unwilling that anyone who is abler than themselves should come into their pulpits, lest they should be more applauded than themselves. A fearful thing it is, that any man, who hath the least of the fear of God, should so envy God's gifts, and had rather that his carnal hearers should remain unconverted, and the drowsy unawakened, than that it should be done by another who may be preferred before him.

Yea, so far doth this cursed vice prevail, that in great congregations, which have need of the help of many preachers, we can scarcely, in many places, get two of equality to live together in love and quietness, and unanimously to carry on the work of God. But unless one of them be quite below the other in parts, and content to be so esteemed, or unless he be a curate to the other, and ruled by him, they are contending for precedency, and envying each other's interest, and walking with strangeness and jealousy towards one another, to the shame of their profession, and the great wrong of their people.

I am ashamed to think of it, that when I have been laboring to convince persons of public interest and capacity, of the great necessity of more ministers than one in large congregations, they tell me, they will never agree together. I hope the objection is unfounded as to the most, but it is a sad case that it should be true of any. Nay, some men are so far gone in pride, that when they might have an equal assistant to further the work of God, they had rather take all the burden upon themselves, though more than they can bear, than that anyone should share with them in the honor, or that their interest in the esteem of the people should be diminished.

Hence also it is that men do so magnify their own opinions, and are as censorious of any that differ from them in lesser things, as if it were all one to differ from them and from God. They expect that all should conform to their judgment, as if they were the rulers of the Church's faith; and while we cry down papal infallibility, too many of us would be popes ourselves, and have all stand to our determination, as if we were infallible. It is true, we have more modesty than expressly to say so. We pretend that it is only the evidence of truth in our reasons, that we expect men should yield to, and our zeal is the truth and not for ourselves.

But as that must needs be taken for truth which is ours, so our reasons must needs be taken for valid. And if they be but freely examined and be found fallacious, as we are exceedingly backward to see it ourselves because they are ours, so we are angry that it should be disclosed to others. We so espouse the cause of our errors, as if all that were spoken against them were spoken against our persons, and we were heinously injured to have our arguments thoroughly confuted, by which we injured the truth and the souls of men. The matter is come to this pass through our pride, that if an error or fallacious argument do fall under the patronage of a reverend name (which is nothing rare), we must either allow it the victory and give away the truth, or else become injurious to that name that doth patronize it.

For though you meddle not with their persons, yet do they put themselves under all the strokes which you give their arguments; and feel them as sensibly as if you had spoken of themselves, because they think it will follow in the eyes of others, that weak arguing is a sign of a weak man. If, therefore, you consider it your duty to shame their errors and false reasonings by discovering their nakedness, they take it as if you shamed their persons. And so their names must be a garrison or fortress to their mistakes, and their reverence must defend all their sayings from attack.

So high indeed are our spirits, that when it becomes the duty of anyone to reprove or contradict us, we are commonly impatient both of the matter and the manner. We love the man who will say as we say, and be of our opinion, and promote our reputation, though in other respects, he be less worthy of our esteem. But he is ungrateful to us who contradicteth us and differeth from us, and dealeth plainly with us as to our miscarriages and telleth us of our faults.

Especially in the management of our public arguings, where the eye of the world is upon us, we can scarcely endure any contradiction or plain dealing. I know that railing language is to be abhorred, and that we should be as tender of each other's reputation, as our fidelity to the truth will permit But our pride makes too many of us think all men condemn us, that do not admire us, yea, and admire all we say, and submit their judgments to our most palpable mistakes. We are so tender that a man can scarcely touch us but we are hurt. We are so high-minded that a man who is not versed in complimenting and skilled in flattery above the vulgar rate can scarcely tell how to handle us so observantly-and fit our expectations at every turnwhithout there being some word or some neglect which our high spirits will fasten on and take as injurious to our honor.

I confess I have often wondered that this most heinous sin should be made so light of, and thought so consistent with a holy frame of heart and life, when far less sins are by ourselves, proclaimed to be so damnable in our people And I have wondered more, to see the difference between godly preachers and ungodly sinners, in this respect. When we speak to drunkards, worldlings, or ignorant unconverted persons, we disgrace them to the utmost, and lay it on as plainly as we can speak, and tell them of their sin, and shame, and misery; and we expect that they should not only bear all patiently, but take all thankfully.

And most that I deal with do take it patiently; and many gross sinners will commend the closest preachers most, and will say that they care not for hearing a man that will not tell then, plainly of their sins. But if we speak to godly ministers against their errors or their sins, if we do not honor them and reverence them, and speak as smoothly as we are able to speak, yea, if we mix not commendations with our reproofs, and if the applause be not predominant, so as to drown all the force of the reproof or confutation, they take it as almost an insufferable injury.

Brethren, I know this is a sad confession, but that all this should exist among us, should be more grievous to us than to be told of it. Could the evil be hid, I should not have disclosed it, at least so openly in the view of all. But, alas, it is long ago open to the eyes of the world. We have dishonored ourselves by idolizing our honor; we print our shame, and preach our shame, thus proclaiming it to the whole world.

Some will think that I speak overcharitably when I call such persons godly men, in whom so great a sin doth so much prevail. I know, indeed, that where it is predominant, not hated, and bewailed, and mortified in the main, there can be no true godliness; and I beseech every man to exercise a strict jealousy and search of

17

his own heart. But if all be graceless that are guilty of any, or of most of the fore-mentioned discoveries of pride, the Lord be merciful to the ministers of this land, and give us quickly another spirit, for grace is then a rarer thing than most of us have supposed it to be.

Yet I must needs say, that I do not mean to involve all the ministers of Christ in this charge. To the praise of Divine grace be it spoken, we have some among us who are eminent for humility and meekness, and who, in these respects, are exemplary to their flocks and to their brethren. It is their glory, and shall be their glory; and maketh them truly honorable and lovely in the eyes of God and of all good men, and even in the eyes of the ungodly themselves. O that the rest of us were but such! But, alas, this is not the case with all of us.

O that the Lord would lay us at his feet in the tears of unfeigned sorrow for this sin! Brethren, may I expostulate this case a little with my own heart and yours, that we may see the evil of our sin, and be reformed! Is not pride the sin of devils, the first-born of hell? Is it not that wherein Satan's image doth much consist? And is it to be tolerated in men who are so engaged against him and his kingdom as we are?

The very design of the gospel is to abase us, and the work of grace is begun and carried on in humiliation. Humility is not a mere ornament of a Christian, but an essential part of the new creature. It is a contradiction in terms, to be a Christian, and not humble. All who will be Christians must be Christ's disciples, and 'come to him to learn'; and the lesson which he teacheth then, is, to 'be meek and lowly.' Oh, how many precepts and admirable examples hath our Lord and Master given us to this end. 'Can we behold him washing and wiping his servants' feet, and yet be proud and lordly still? Shall he converse with the meanest of the people, and shall we avoid them as below our notice, and think none but persons of wealth and honor fit for our society? How many of us are oftener found in the houses of gentlemen than in the cottages of the poor, who most need our help?

There are many of us who would think it below us, to be daily with the most needy and beggarly people, instructing them in the way of life and salvation, as if we had taken charge of the souls of the rich only! Alas, what is it that we have to be proud of? Is it of our body? Why, is it not made of the like materials as the brutes, and must it not shortly be as loathsome and abominable as a carcass? Is it of our graces? Why, the more we are proud of them the less we have to be proud of. When so much of the nature of grace consists in humility, it is a great absurdity to be proud of it. Is it of our knowledge and learning? Why, if we have any knowledge at all, we must needs know how much reason we have to be humble; and if we know more than others, how much must more reason than others to be humble.

How little is it that the most learned know, in comparison of that of which they are ignorant! To know that things are past your reach, and to know how ignorant you are, one would think should be no great cause of pride. However, do not the devils know more than you? And will you be proud of that in which the devils excel you? Our very business is to teach the great lesson of humility to our people; and how unfit, then, is it that we should be proud ourselves? We must study humility, and preach humility; and must we not possess and practice humility? A proud preacher of humility is at least a self-condemning man.

What a sad case is it, that so vile a sin is not more easily discerned by us, but many who are most proud can blame it in others, and yet take no notice of it in themselves! The world takes notice of some among us, that they have aspiring minds, and seek for the highest room, and must be the rulers, and bear the sway wherever they come, or else there is no living or acting with them. In any consultations, they come not to search after truth, but to dictate to others? who, perhaps, are fit to teach them. In a word, they have such arrogant domineering spirits, that the world rings of it, and yet they will not see it in themselves!

Brethren, I desire to deal closely with my own heart and yours. I beseech you consider whether it will save us to speak well of the grace of humility while we possess it not, or to speak against the sin of pride while we indulge in it? Have not many of us cause to inquire diligently, whether sincerity will consist with such a measure of pride as we feel? When we are telling the drunkard that he cannot be saved unless he become temperate, and the fornicator that he cannot be saved unless he become chaste, have we not as great reason if we are proud, to say to ourselves, that we cannot be saved unless we become humble?

Pride, in fact, is a greater sin than drunkenness or whoredom; and humility is as necessary as sobriety and chastity. Truly, brethren, a man may as certainly, and more slyly, make haste to hell, in the way of earnest preaching of the gospel, and seeming zeal for a holy life, as in a way of drunkeness and filthiness. For what is holiness, but a devotedness to God and a living to him? And what is a damnable state, but a devotedness to carnal self and a living to ourselves? And doth anyone live more to himself, or less to God, than the proud man? And may not pride make a preacher study for himself and pray and preach, and live to himself, even when he seemeth to surpass others in the work? It is not the work without the right principle and end that will prove us upright. The work may be God's, and yet we may do it, not for God, but for ourselves. I confess I feel such continual danger on this point, that if I do not watch, lest I should study for myself, and preach for myself, and write for myself, rather than for Christ, I should soon miscarry; and after all, I justify not myself, when I must condemn the sin.

Consider, I beseech you, brethren, what baits there are in the work of the ministry to entice a man to selfishness, even in the highest works of piety. The fame of a godly man is as great a snare as the fame of a learned man. But woe to him that takes up the fame of godliness instead of godliness! 'Verily I say unto you, they have their reward.' When the times were all for learning and empty formalities, the temptation of the proud did lie that way. But now, when, through the unspeakable mercy of God, the most lively practical preaching is in credit, and godliness itself is in credit, the temptation of the proud is to pretend to be zealous preachers and godly men.

Oh, what a fine thing is it to have the people crowding to hear us, and affected with what we say, and yielding up to us their judgments and affections! What a taking thing is it to be cried up as the ablest and godliest man in the country, to be famed through the land for the highest spiritual excellencies! Alas, brethren, a little grace combined with such inducements will serve to make you join yourselves with the forwardest in promoting the cause of Christ in the world. Nay, pride may do it without special grace.

Oh, therefore, be jealous of yourselves, and, amidst all your studies, be sure to study humility. 'He that exalteth himself shall be humbled, and he that humbleth himself shall be exalted.' I commonly observe that almost all men, whether good or bad, do loathe the proud, and love the humble. So far indeed doth pride contradict itself, that, conscious of its own deformity, it often borrows the homely dress of humility. We have the more cause to be jealous of it, because it is a sin most deeply rooted in our nature, and as hardly as any extirpated from the soul.

A Word About Pride

Richard Baxter

Richard Baxter

Richard Baxter

Printed in Great Britain
by Amazon

77860590R00020